Your Heart

by Terri DeGezelle

Consultant:
Marjorie Hogan, M.D.
Associate Professor of Pediatrics, University of Minnesota
Pediatrician, Hennepin County Medical Center

Bridgestone Books
an imprint of Capstone Press
Mankato, Minnesota

Bridgestone Books are published by Capstone Press
151 Good Counsel Drive, P.O. Box 669, Mankato, Minnesota 56002
http://www.capstone-press.com

Library of Congress Cataloging-in-Publication Data
DeGezelle, Terri, 1955–
     Your heart/by Terri DeGezelle.
     p. cm.—(Bridgestone science library)
     Includes bibliographical references and index.
     Summary: Introduces the heart, its function within the circulatory system,
heart diseases, and how to keep the heart healthy.
     ISBN 0-7368-1148-6
     1. Heart—Juvenile literature. [1. Heart.] I. Title. II. Series.
QP111.6 .D44 2002
612.1′7—dc21

                                                                    2001003594

Editorial Credits
Rebecca Glaser, editor; Karen Risch, product planning editor; Linda Clavel, cover and
     interior layout designer and illustrator; Alta Schaffer, photo researcher; Nancy White,
     photo stylist

Photo Credits
Capstone Press/Gary Sundermeyer, 4, 20
Diane Meyer, 16
International Stock/Patrick Ramsey, 18
RubberBall Productions, cover (boy)
Unicorn Stock Photos/Jim Hayes Photography, cover (heart models)

1 2 3 4 5 6 07 06 05 04 03 02

Table of Contents

Fun Fact

Your heart is about the
same size as your fist.

Your Heart

The heart is a strong muscle that works like a pump. Your heart pumps blood to all parts of your body. Your heart works all the time. It pumps when you run. It even works while you sleep.

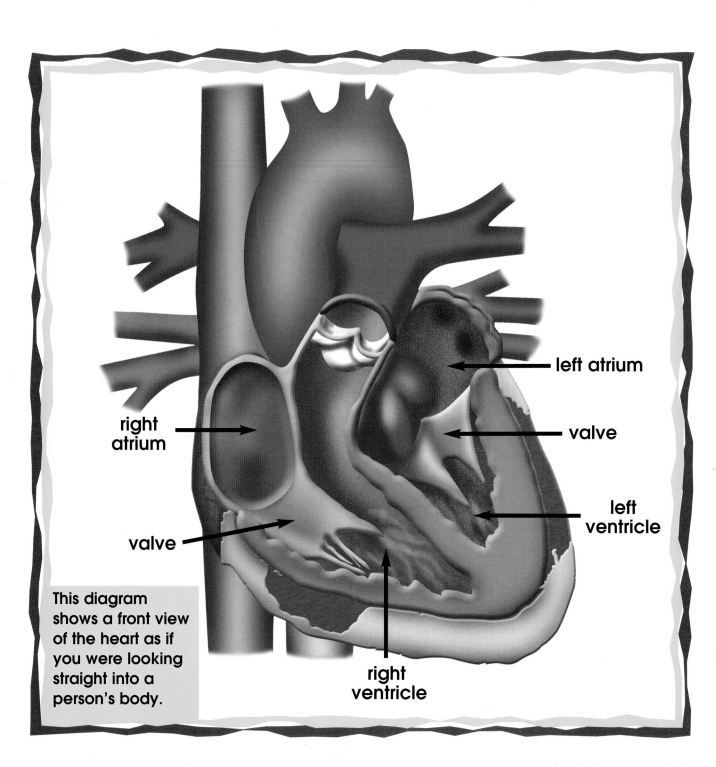

left atrium

valve

left
ventricle

right
atrium

valve

right
ventricle

This diagram shows a front view of the heart as if you were looking straight into a person's body.

Inside Your Heart

Your heart is in the middle of your chest. There are four chambers in your heart. The right side of the heart has a right atrium and a right ventricle. The left atrium and left ventricle are on the left side of the heart. Valves open to let blood flow between the chambers.

chamber
a space inside something

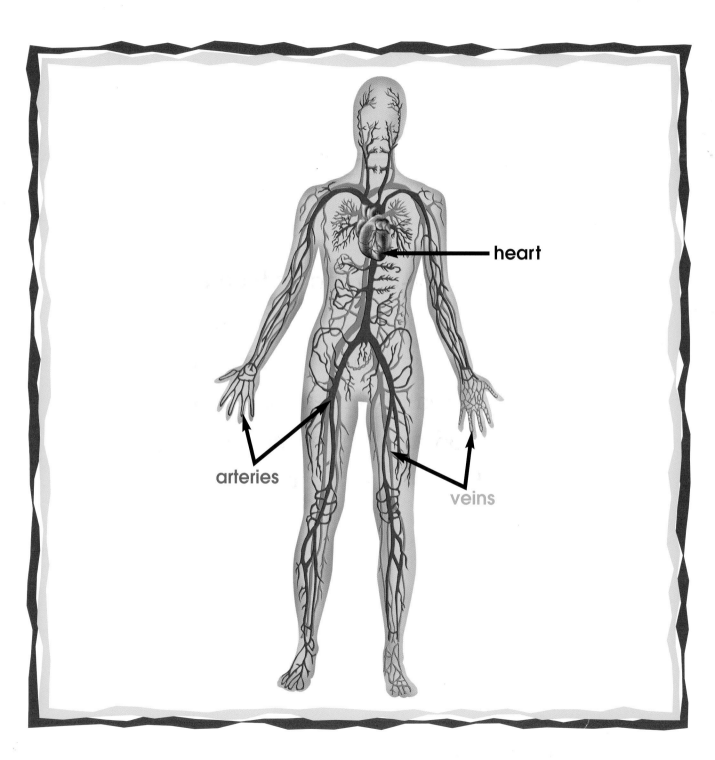

heart

arteries

veins

Your Circulatory System

The circulatory system carries blood to all parts of your body. The heart, arteries, veins, and blood make up the circulatory system. Arteries are tubes that carry blood away from the heart. Veins are tubes that carry blood back to the heart.

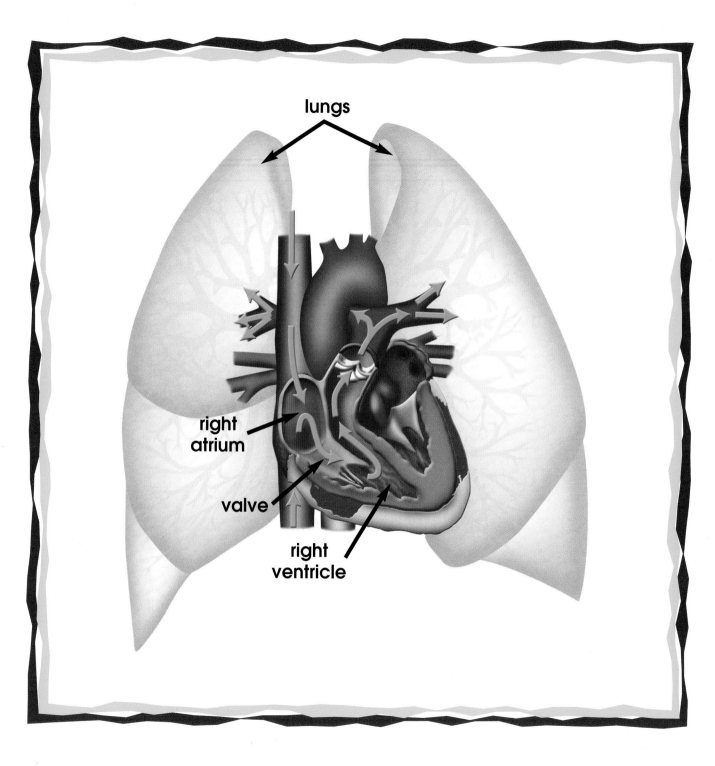

lungs

right
atrium

valve

right
ventricle

Blood Enters the Heart

Blood enters the heart through the right atrium. The valves open and blood flows through. The valves close to keep the blood from flowing backward. The blood then flows into the right ventricle. The right ventricle pumps the blood to the lungs.

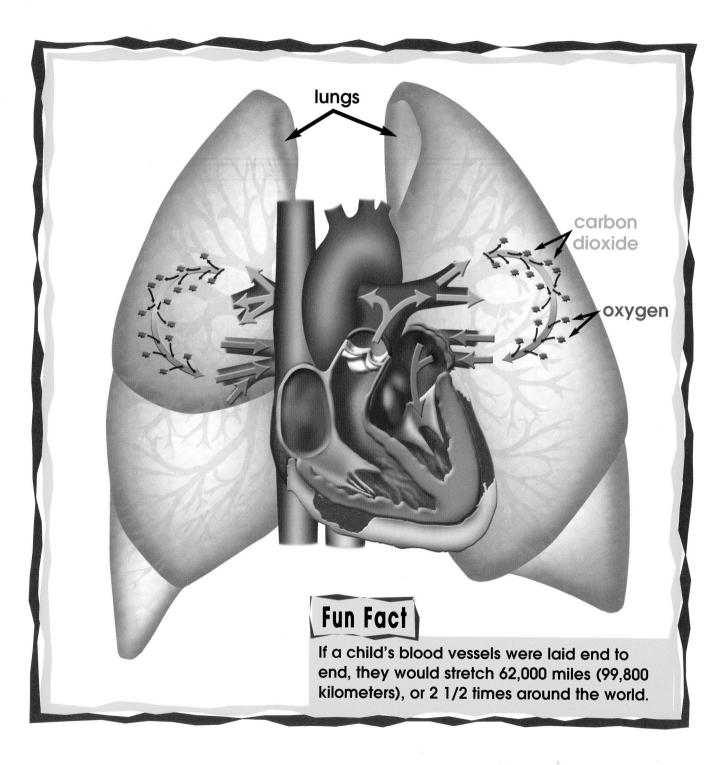

lungs

carbon dioxide

oxygen

Fun Fact

If a child's blood vessels were laid end to end, they would stretch 62,000 miles (99,800 kilometers), or 2 1/2 times around the world.

Blood Travels through the Lungs

Blood flows from the right side of the heart to the lungs. The blood leaves carbon dioxide in the lungs and picks up oxygen. Oxygen is in the air you breathe. Veins from the lungs bring blood with oxygen back to the heart.

carbon dioxide
a colorless gas that people breathe out

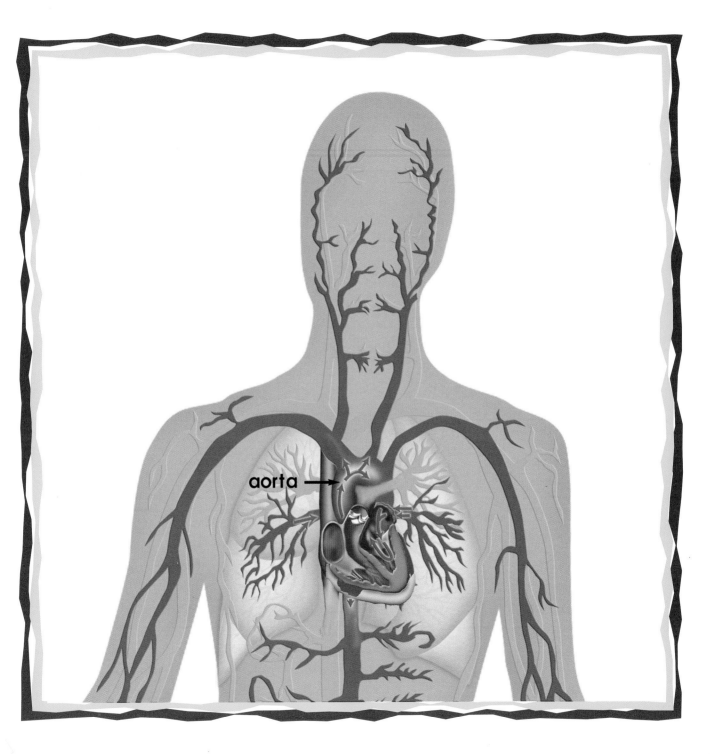

aorta

The Heart Pumps the Blood Out

Blood from the lungs enters the left atrium and goes to the left ventricle. The left ventricle pumps blood out through the aorta. The aorta branches into smaller arteries that carry blood to all parts of your body. Veins carry blood back to the heart. The cycle starts again.

aorta
the main artery that carries blood away from the heart

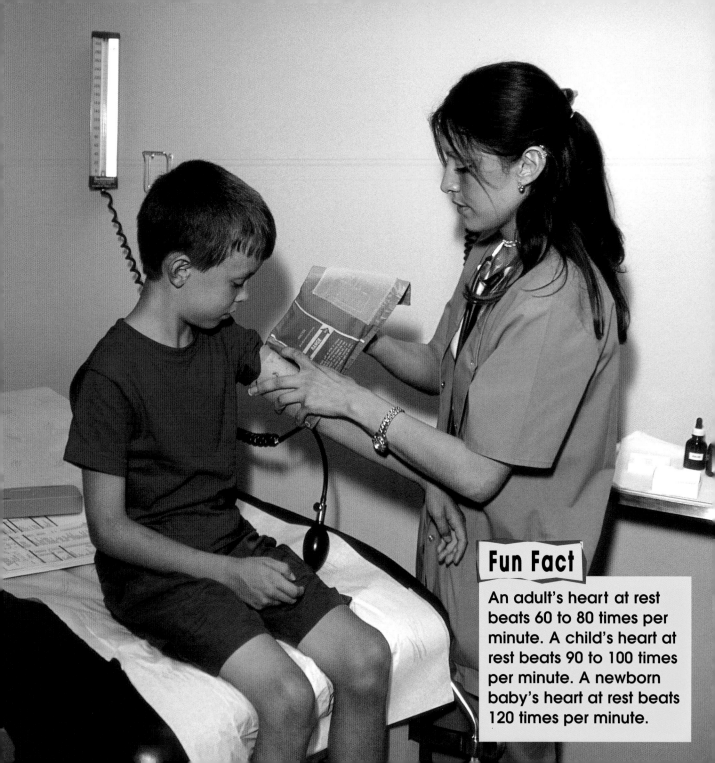

Fun Fact

An adult's heart at rest beats 60 to 80 times per minute. A child's heart at rest beats 90 to 100 times per minute. A newborn baby's heart at rest beats 120 times per minute.

Your Pulse and Blood Pressure

Blood moving through your body is your pulse. Your pulse becomes faster when you exercise because you need more oxygen. The heart pumps faster to get more blood to all body parts. Your blood pressure goes up when you exercise or get excited.

blood pressure
the force of blood pushing against artery and vein walls

Fun Fact

Doctors can tell how healthy
your heart is by listening to your
heartbeat with a stethoscope.

Heart Attacks and Diseases

A cardiologist is a doctor who treats heart diseases. These doctors may treat people who have heart attacks. They also see people who have blocked arteries. Children born with heart problems are also patients of cardiologists.

heart attack

when an artery near the heart becomes blocked and the heart does not get enough oxygen

A Healthy Heart

You can keep your heart healthy. Exercise will make your heart stronger. Eating foods low in fat keeps your arteries clear. Staying away from cigarette smoke also is good for your heart.

Hands On: Check Your Friend's Pulse

What You Need

A friend
Stopwatch
Paper and pencil

What You Do

1. Have your friend sit quietly for a few minutes.
2. Place your first two fingers gently on the inside part of your friend's wrist, just below the thumb. Do not use your thumb because it has its own pulse.
3. Set the stopwatch for one minute. Count the number of beats you feel in one minute.
4. Write down that number.
5. Have your friend run in place for one minute.
6. Have your friend sit down. Check your friend's pulse again for one minute.
7. Write that number down. Which number is higher?
8. Switch places with your friend and repeat steps 1 through 7.

Your pulse is faster after you exercise. Your muscles need extra oxygen when you are active. Your heart must work harder and faster to pump blood throughout your body.

Words to Know

aorta (ay-OR-tuh)—the largest artery in your body; the aorta carries blood away from your heart.

artery (AR-tuh-ree)—a tube that carries blood away from the heart to all parts of the body

atrium (AY-tree-uhm)—one of the chambers in the top of the heart that receives blood from veins

blood vessel (BLUHD VESS-uhl)—a tube that carries blood through your body; arteries and veins are blood vessels.

oxygen (AHK-suh-juhn)—a colorless gas in the air that people need to live

valve (VALV)—a movable part in the heart that controls the flow of blood

vein (VAYN)—a tube that carries blood back to the heart

ventricle (VEN-tri-kuhl)—one of the chambers in the bottom of the heart that pumps blood out through the arteries

Read More

Hurst, J. Willis, and Stuart D. Hurst. *The Heart: The Kids' Question and Answer Book.* New York: McGraw-Hill, 1999.

LeVert, Suzanne. *The Heart.* Kaleidoscope. New York: Benchmark Books/Marshall Cavendish, 2001.

Vander Hook, Sue. *Heart Disease.* Understanding Illness. Mankato, Minn.: Smart Apple Media, 2000.

Internet Sites

All About The Heart
http://kidshealth.org/kid/body/heart_noSW.html
The Life Pump—The Circulatory System
http://www.imcpl.org/kids_circ.htm
Your Gross and Cool Body—Cardiovascular System
http://yucky.kids.discovery.com/noflash/body/pg000131.html

Index